Economic, Political

and Social History

of Puerto Rico

From 1898 to 1990

M. E. Brandon

Prologue

This book intends to go deeper into the recent history of Puerto Rico trying to offer answers to some historical questions while providing a detailed vision of the social, economic and political evolution of the Caribbean island.

The idea of writing on Puerto Rico's modern history emerged while coursing postgraduate studies specialized in the United States Foreign Policy and, almost by chance, I became familiar with the particular status of the Island.

My personal interest pushed me to develop an extensive project for which it was necessary the compilation of a vast amount of information from a wide bibliography including official documents published by different governments and international organizations. This information resulted indispensable at the moment of sculpted a detailed and clear image of the events that have taken place in Puerto Rico from the arrival of the United States until now.

INDEX

Chapter 1: Introduction

Geographically, Puerto Rico belongs to the Caribbean. Culturally, it is part of the community of Hispanic American peoples. Politically and economically, it is intimately associated with the United States. These three points of reference-and especially a political status of free association-are the points of departure for defining Puerto Rico's place in the world and its relationship with other countries[i].

On July 25, 1898, after over four centuries of Spanish rule, the small Caribbean island of Puerto Rico became a possession of the United Sates. From then on the American Congress would confront the dilemma of which kind of status it should grant to its new territorial possession.

At first, American officials decided to "Americanise" the island and its inhabitants in order to prepare them for statehood.

The United States imposed on Puerto Ricans the learning of the English language and the American government system and laws while remodelling the island's welfare by building hundreds of schools and hospitals and by improving its infrastructure.

In social terms, the new industries were not able to completely absorb the constantly growing labour force and the Puerto Rican government resolved that encouraging migration to the mainland was the solution to the labour surplus.

From 1940 to 1980, hundreds of thousands of poor Puerto Ricans settled on the mainland, especially in New York, in the hope of finding a better future for themselves and their families.

Once there, besides having to adapt to a different culture and language, Puerto Ricans found themselves part of the poorest community in the United States and belonging to a racially discriminated against ethnic minority and, even worse, they felt isolated from the reality of the island.

By the 1950s, the Americans realised that they would never mould Puerto Ricans into their own image and "Americanisation" was dropped from the political agenda.

The resistance shown by the inhabitants of Puerto Rico to accept the "American life style" provoked the abandonment of the "Americanization" process and its withdrawal from the political agenda of Washington.

In addition, many people on the mainland never considered statehood an option as they regarded Puerto Rico as far too poor and Spanish to become part of the Union.

On the other hand, the United States did not contemplate independence as a viable alternative as there was a spread belief that Puerto Ricans, and most of Latin Americans, were no able to govern themselves.

The answer to the puzzle came in 1952 when, after a popular referendum backing it, the Commonwealth of Puerto Rico was proclaimed. This new status was expected to grant the island with social and political autonomy and many of the island's inhabitants considered it as the first step towards independence.

These notions, nevertheless, were mistaken and Puerto Ricans found themselves without a voice on any aspect of the political, social and economic life of the island without previously consulting and gaining the consent of the United States Congress.

Throughout the years, the United States has refused to implement any real change in the Commonwealth compact, converting the status question into the most frustrating issue in Puerto Ricans' lives and spreading criticism among the international community.

At the same time, the island's economy became increasingly dependent on the mainland for its survival.

This dependence was even greater when, from 1941, the Puerto Rican government implemented an economic recovery plan. The main feature of this program was the introduction of industrial tax exemptions, which converted Puerto Rico into a tax-free paradise attracting both United States' investments and tourists.

The industrial development brought with it a neglect of the island's agriculture with a consequent loss of jobs in that sector.

As a result of foreign investment, the development of local industry was neglected while the big American chains, television and radio stations exercised a constant cultural bombardment on the island's society.

At the meantime, migration to the mainland has been somewhat alleviated but has neither resolved the problem of labour surplus nor reduced the high unemployment rate in the island. On the contrary, migration created a dispersal of the Puerto Rican society.

By 1980, and although social services and infrastructure had improved impressively, the island continued to be overpopulated. A great number of its inhabitants were surviving on federal aid and many of them were living in the several slums that surrounded Puerto Rico's capital, San Juan.

Chapter 2: Historical Background

In the autumn of 1897, a liberal government took over in Spain and granted autonomy to the few territorial possessions that the country had managed to retain on the other side of the Atlantic: Cuba and Puerto Rico.

The Puerto Rican Chapter of Autonomy, which was proclaimed on November 25, 1897, offered Puerto Rico representation in the Spanish Parliament, Las Cortes. It granted Puerto Rico with a civil Governor appointed by the Spanish Parliament.

Furthermore, the Chapter introduced a two-chamber legislature: the Upper Chamber or Administrative Council, formed by 15 members, eight of whom were appointed by the Governor, and the Lower House or Chamber of Representatives, elected by the people for a 5-year period[ii].

Puerto Rico would participate in international treaties between Spain and a third country on matters affecting the island and had the right to veto any decision on the island taken by the Spanish parliament, as well as the right to fix its own tariffs[iii].

The long awaited Autonomy entered into effect on July 17, 1898, just eight days before the United States took over the Caribbean island and swept away the Chapter of Autonomy.

At the time of their arrival in Puerto Rico, on July 25, 1898, the Americans found a small country with almost a million inhabitants, most of them living in poverty.

The island had a serious lack of mineral resources, only possessed small amounts of iron, copper and manganese, and had a mountainous demography that left only a small portion of the land, around 27%, suitable for its cultivation with only 10% being highly productive[iv].

The diversification of the agriculture was reduced to a few crops such as, sugar, coffee and tobacco, and some fruits and vegetables, such as bananas, pineapples and potatoes.

The industrial sector was basically non-existent being limited to a few needlework plants, some clothing and food factories and a small number of beer manufacturers.

The country's wealth was also poorly distributed and the island had a semi-feudal society with a small educated upper class and a huge mass of terrible poor inhabitants. The illiteracy level was high and living and health conditions were dreadful.

At first, hoping for economic and political improvements, Puerto Ricans received the new rulers with great expectations. The United States was a country of freedom and prosperity and the islanders believed that America would develop a democratic self-government system in Puerto Rico, which could prepare the island for independence.

However, the United States had no intention of granting self-government to the island as the Americans regarded Puerto Ricans as inferior beings not suitable to decide their own destiny and conduct their own politics.

The result was that the Americans tried to prepare the island for statehood by sweeping away its culture and style of life. There was widespread belief among American officials that a different culture was a backward one and that the only chance that a country had to prosper was to copy the "American way."

The United States thus tried to "Americanise" Puerto Ricans by improving living conditions in the island.

For instance, between 1898 and 1920, almost 6,000 miles of roads were built[v]. American values were also spread through education. As a result, hundreds of schools were established in mountainous and isolated towns while in 1903, the University of Puerto Rico was founded while ten years later, in 1913, two private universities, the Catholic University and the Inter-American University, opened their doors. During that period, government expenditures on education grew from 20% to 42% while the number of children at the school increased from 7% to 37%[vi].

Americans also attempted to "Americanise" Puerto Ricans through the passing of the Foraker Act that installed American laws and government system on the island while imposing the learning of the English language on the population.

Chapter 3: The Political Framework up to 1940

Political Background: The Foraker Act

On April 12, 1900, after a series of military governors who showed little sensitivity to the Puerto Rican culture and values, the Congress passed the Organic Act of Puerto Rico, known as the Foraker Act after its mentor Senator Joseph Foraker of Ohio. The Act passed into effect on May 1, 1900 and it defined the government system of the island.

It introduced an Upper House formed by 11 members appointed by the President of the United States, five of them Puerto Ricans, and a 35-member-strong elected Lower House.

The Act called for a civil Governor, appointed by the President of the United States, who possessed a right of veto over any law approved by the Puerto Rican legislature.

The United States extended its monetary system to the island, set the American tax system in the island and, from 1902 onwards, free trade between Puerto Rico and the United States was made possible[vii]. Judicial power would lie in the Supreme Court of Puerto Rico whose members were appointed by the American President.

It was not longer before disillusionment took root among the island's population as the Foraker Act extensively reduced the degree of autonomy that Puerto Rico had enjoyed just before America's arrival.

A good example of this is that under the Spanish Chapter of Autonomy, Puerto Rico was allowed to send 24 representatives with the right to vote to the Spanish Parliament[viii].

Under the Foraker Act, Puerto Rico was entitled to send a representative to Washington, Resident Commissioner, who could participate in congressional debates but not vote. Under the Spanish Chapter, Puerto Ricans were Spanish citizens with all their rights.

Under the Foraker Act, they were granted neither a Bill of Rights nor citizenship, being named citizens of Puerto Rico under the protection of the United States.

Spain had allowed Puerto Ricans to set their own duties on products entering the island and to participate in international treaties affecting Puerto Rico. The United States, on the other hand, set the island's tariff and controlled its foreign policy.

The biggest disappointment was the imposition of English as the language of instruction at the island's schools and children who could not understand any English began to be taught the language by teachers who hardly could speak it.

The measure had the opposite effect to that intended by its American mentors, and instead of converting Puerto Ricans into English-speaking people the decision alienated the island's population.

Puerto Ricans came to regard the Spanish language as an important part of their inheritance and identity and fought to restore it as the island's official language.

In 1900, the islanders achieved a small victory when Spanish was made the language of instruction in the primary schools, a decision that was reverted five years later, in 1905 when English became the main language, once more. In 1916, Spanish again became the main language from grades one to four, with both languages taught in 5th grade and English the language of instruction from grade 6^{ix} and beyond.

Political Background: The Jones Act

Puerto Rican politicians started to press Washington for the introduction of some changes that would grant more autonomy to the island.

These pressures eventually had some results when, in March 1917, the Jones Act, named after its creator, Congressman William A. Jones of Virginia, was passed by Congress and signed by President Woodrow Wilson[x].

The Bill granted American citizenship to the people of Puerto Rico and converted the 35-elected members Lower House into a 39-member one, and the presidential- appointed Upper House into an elected 19-member Senate.

Nevertheless, the United States President and Congress maintained absolute power over the Puerto Rican legislature. In addition, many Puerto Ricans were furious about the citizenship clause, feeling that Congress had imposed American citizenship on them as its refusal would result in the loss of some important rights, such as the right to vote, the right to apply for state jobs and the right to hold a passport.

The Foraker and Jones Acts had modelled the Puerto Rican government and education system, laws, trade, and foreign policy in the American image.

However, by the 1940s, Americans finally realised that Puerto Rico was different to any other territory that the United States had taken over.

Unlike Hawaii and Alaska there was no American community settled in previously to the United States' arrival. Unlike some other states that at the time of joining the Union had a majority Spanish population, such as California and New Mexico, the Caribbean island was an old and overpopulated country, set in its ways, with a deep-rooted culture and values, which often entered into conflict with those of the United States.

By then, transforming Puerto Rico into a commonwealth state was contemplated as the solution to the island's status.

Chapter 4: Economic and Social Development in Puerto Rico up to

1898-1940

In 1898, the United States realised that the boosting of Puerto Rican economy passed for recreating a new economy and social system that could replace to the old fashion models established on the island.

The old style paternalistic small farms where employees and employers worked together as a family unit, typical of the Spanish period, were transformed into big corporations with heavy machinery and absentee owners.

As a consequence, small farmers were pushed out while big firms accumulated all the cultivable land.

By 1930, although in 1900 the Foraker Act included a 500-Acre Land Law that prohibited any corporation from controlling more than 500 acres of land, four big American corporations: The South Porto Rico Sugar Company, the Fajardo Sugar Company, Central Aguirre associates and the United Puerto Rico Sugar Company, controlled over 50% of the sugar cultivated and over 40% of the agricultural wealth of the island[xi].

Overall, American businesses owned 60% of the sugar industry converting the island into a mono-agricultural society as crops that had been extensively cultivated before the Americans' arrival, such as rice and coffee were ignored for the sake of sugar production.

The economic situation worsened when the economical depression created by the Wall Street Crash of October 1929, had catastrophic consequences on the island.

The New Deal Reaches Puerto Rico

The economic situation of Puerto Rico was so dramatic that, by the year 1933, the American President, Franklin D. Roosevelt, decided to extend his New Deal policy to the island.

For the next five years, the United States spent nearly $60 million on Puerto Rico's reconstruction[xii] through the establishment of Federal agencies settled up to bring economic relief to the population.

In this way, the Farm Credit Administration and the Agriculture Adjustment Agency, which conducted agrarian research and granted loans to individual farmers, were established in 1933.

That same year, the Puerto Rican Emergency Relief Administration (PRERA) a subsidiary of the Federal Emergency Relief Administration, started to operate.

PRERA's aims were to fight unemployment and to develop a food distribution programme. By 1934, although around 35% of Puerto Ricans had received some kind of aid from PRERA, the agency failed to resolve the long- term economic and social problems.

The Chardón Plan

The incapacity if the PRERA for solving the economic problems of Puerto Rico forced the Chancellor of the University of Puerto Rico, Carlos Chardón, to develop a plan, which was approved by the American Congress in June 1934 and which aim was the agrarian reform. The so-called Chardón Plan consisted of the setting up of a semi-public firm that could enforce the 500-Acre Law and distribute land among the poor.

The agency, the Puerto Rico Recovery Administration (PRRA) was established in 1935 and made responsible for the purchasing of land and the resettlement of families.

One year after its foundation, in 1936, the PRRA had bought over 10,000 acres for redistribution, as well as a sugar mill, the Central Lafayette. Furthermore, in 1938, the PRRA set up the Farm Security Administration that helped tenants to purchase farms. By 1943, the PRRA had established over 12,400 farms[xiii] while pursuing lawsuits against big corporations that did not respect the 500-acres Land Law.

By 1940, the PRRA's success had been insufficient to pull Puerto Rico out of its economic stagnation and it was clear that the government's efforts on land reform were not producing the expected results with around 40 corporations still holding a total of 250,000 acres of land and almost 60% of the cultivable land was owned by little more than 5% of farms[xiv].

To worsen things, by 1940, the only source of wealth on the island, the sugar industry, entered into competition with Cuba and the Dominican Republic's sugar.

Social Situation in Puerto Rico by 1940

By the decade of the 1940s, social conditions in Puerto Rico had not experienced significant improvements. Income distribution was still skewed; while Puerto Rico's lower class amounted to 86% of the population, it received less than 30% of the island's total income, while more than 70% of Puerto Rico's income was distributed among the small upper and middle-class sectors[xv].

The island's population, now supported by improvements in welfare, continued growing at an alarming rate, from little more than 950,000 inhabitants in 1899 to almost 1,870,000 in 1940[xvi].

Housing conditions were dreadful and, although by 1940 the PRRA had spent around $10 million on housing projects, only 28% of housing had electric power, 21% running water and 14% a toilet[xvii] while the slums surrounded San Juan were extending.

Something needed to be done and President Roosevelt thought that a New Dealer, Rexford Tugwell, could resolve the problem of the Puerto Rican economy. In 1940, Tugwell was named governor of Puerto Rico. He would be the last and best American governor to the island.

Chapter 5: The Beginning of Puerto Rico's Economic Development

From the day of his arrival, Tugwell understood that in order to pull Puerto Rico out of its financial stagnation, the island's economic and social partners had to be reshaped.

His ideas were shared by the leader of the dominant Popular Democratic Party and major figure in Puerto Rican politics, Luis Muñoz Marín. Both men worked together in putting their proposals into practice.

As a result, in 1941, a plan of industrial development that called for the improvement of public services and the creation of a basic socio-economic infrastructure was implemented.

The plan concentrated on agrarian reform and an Agricultural Development Company was set up with the objective of stimulating improvement in technology and conducting research focused on creating a more diversified agricultural sector.

More important, a Land Authority was established as an agency of the Department of Agriculture and Commerce with the aim of purchasing and expropriating the land held by corporations that had violated the 500-Acres Land Law and which will be distributed and converted into subsistence farms and co-operatives.

The Land Authority proved to be very successful and, by 1945, it had allocated over 13,000 plots to families and it has set up a Planning Board to regulate the use of urban land, as well as it acquired and operated some sugar mills.

After World War II, the Planning Board's activities focused on improving factories, schools, transportation facilities, telephone and power supplies and clearing the slums, among other activities.

During the decade of the 1940s, other agencies also opened their doors like the Water Resources Authority, established to provide electricity power to Puerto Rico; the Transportation Authority that was in charge of facilitating communications; and the Aqueduct and Sewer Authority which was established to provide water to the island.

The Establishment of Fomento and its Influence in Industrial Development

From the late 1930s, the Chilean government had encouraged industrial development by creating the Chile's "Corporación de Fomento de la Producción" through which public money was used to improve the Chilean infrastructure, welfare and industrial sector. Puerto Rican officials inspired by Chile's example decided to extend development stimulation to the manufacturing sector.

In 1942, the Puerto Rican Industrial Development Company (PRIDCO) was set up to replace the PRRA and became popularly known as Fomento.

PRIDCO's aims were assist local enterprises in the all the phases of industrial development from research and marketing to promotional assistance.

Fomento purchased and operated different enterprises. For instance, the agency acquired a glass bottle factory, a rum plant, cardboard and shoes and leather factories and a very successful cement plant.

Fomento also purchased several factories that manufactured cotton and furniture, and some textile and hosiery knitting mills, as well as did diamond cutting.

Additionally, it founded the Products Design Division in charge of the manufacturing of ceramic products, rugs, bamboo and wooden furniture.

In 1945, it launched the Puerto Rico Lay Products Corporation to produce tiles and ceramic goods and, in 1947, PRIDCO, started the construction of the island's first hotel, the luxury Caribe Hilton.

To assist Fomento and its new industries with their finances, the Puerto Rican government set up the Government Development Bank which between 1944 and 1957 approved loans for near $40 million for industrial buildings[xviii].

The Social Activities of Fomento

Parts of the activities of PRIDCO (Fomento) were to improve social conditions and reduce the high unemployment rate on the island. In pursuit of these aims, it conducted educational training among the unemployed and sent graduates to the United States to obtain work experience.

Same improvement's measures were also introduced in the labour sector like the approval of a Minimum Wage Law, in 1941, and a Child-Labour Law, in 1942, which prohibited the employment of under 16's and reduced working hours to 40 a week. In 1943, the Mediation and Coalition Service was established to help workers and employers reach agreements in labour disputes.

To anyone curious about the process of rapid economic growth, Puerto Rico provides a most interesting case. It has dramatically overcome those obstacles often cited as the reasons why other regions advance slowly or not at all: scarcity of skilled labour and natural resources, heavy dependence on one crop for income and exports, and a shortage of domestic capital[xix].

By 1947, although Fomento has grown from its initial value of $0.5 million to more than $22 million[xx], its success was limited. Only a small portion of large corporations had been affected by the redistribution of land while some of the public protected farms were not providing benefits. Furthermore, Fomento had been able to generate only 2,000 jobs accounting for around 1% of the employment needed on the island and, at the same time, the Puerto Rican labour force was increasing by an average of 10,000 workers a year[xxi].

Chapter 6: Operation Bootstrap

The planners of the Puerto Rican rehabilitation efforts realised that public investment was not enough to input to the island economy and resolved that the solution to the problem lay in allowing private investment while shifting attention from agriculture to industry.

The result was a series of measures, designed by the Popular Democratic Party and popularly known as Operation Bootstrap that attracted foreign, mainly American, investment to the island.

In 1947, the Puerto Rican legislature began the island's industrial development by approving the Industrial Incentives Act that exempted new industries from income and property taxes for a 10 year-period and which, in 1954, was extended for a further 10-years period. To provide protection for the Industrial Incentives Act, the Industrial Tax Exemption was created.

The Establishment of the EDA

As part of the Operation Bootstrap, in 1950, Fomento-owned enterprises were sold to the private sector while the agency implemented its activities being renamed the Economic Development Administration (EDA) and inheriting 66 plants and all PRIDCO's agencies.

The EDA's tasks were to produce both short and long-term plans, to undertake industrial research and to manage the activities of the development program. The EDA consisted of a series of agencies such as the Office of Economic Research (OER), which analysed future targets and provided legal advice.

The EDA also had an Industrial Development branch, which dealt with promotional campaigns to encourage investments, and assisted businessmen with business start-up problems.

The branch included the Industrial Development Company that dealt, among others things, with the granting of loans to new industrial enterprises and the renting of industrial buildings and a Department of Tourism to promote tourist activities.

The next step was the construction of an infrastructure that matched the transportation and communication needs of the new industries. In 1948, the Puerto Rico Ports Authority was founded to deal with trade issues. In addition, miles of roads and railways were constructed, while the San Juan International Airport opened its doors in 1948.

Operation Bootstrap also provided adequate labour force to the industry sector. Therefore, the EDA founded the Accelerated Industrial Training Program to provide short and long-term training for the large number of Puerto Rico's unskilled unemployed. The EDA also underwent the construction of vocational schools throughout the island, hiring teachers and technicians from the mainland.

In 1949, President Truman launched his Point Four Program, which consisted in sending technicians to train workers in underdeveloped areas. Muñoz Marín was prompted to offer Puerto Rico as a training centre for new techniques in economic development, education, health and planning. The program became known as the Puerto Rico Planning Board enjoying great international popularity with students from more than 100 different countries participating in the courses.

However, Puerto Rico was an overpopulated island with a considerable labour force's surplus and the new industries opened under the government's protection could absorb part of that labour surplus but not all of it. If Operation Bootstrap was to have the slightest chance of success, the island had to control its population.

The government tried to resolve the problem by encouraging Puerto Ricans to reduce the size of their families. With this objective in mind, in 1948, the Family Planning Association was founded offering free information and contraceptives.

The government also tried to reduce the island's population through emigration setting, in 1943, the Civil Aeronautics Board that fetched regular and cheap flights between Puerto Rico's capital, San Juan, and New York City.

The exploitation of the tourist industry was another of Operation Bootstrap's features and, by 1969, the tourist industry was generating around $230,000 million per annum and employed over 10,000 people catering for the more than 1 million tourists who visited the island[xxii].

The result was a massive wave of American investment that literally swamped the island. Besides exemption from income and property taxes, American businesses found other advantages in Puerto Rico. For instance, the Jones Act of 1917 had exempted Puerto Rico from federal taxes and provided the Caribbean Island with common citizenship, currency and a market, which created a favourable climate for United States' investment.

Finally, the political stability enjoyed by Puerto Rico, with the pro-Commonwealth Popular Party dominating local politics, its closeness to the mainland and the numerous improvements in infrastructure and labour education implemented by the island's government, together with the prospect of a cheap labour force, worked as a magnet for American businesses.

The EDA's success record was impressive and although by 1950 the industry sector engaged only 9% of the labour force; in 1960, it absorbed 35% of workers[xxiii]. Additionally, personal income grew from $218 per capita per annum in 1940 to $804 in 1967. In the same period, national income increased from $407 million to $2,163 million while employment decreased by 28%[xxiv].

Operation Bootstrap's Educational Programme

From the earlier 1960s, Puerto Rican development efforts had become a model for other underdeveloped areas.

As a result, in 1960, the Caribbean Training Program sponsored by the Puerto Rican government and the United States International Co-operation Administration, was set up to organise courses for students, from undeveloped countries, in Puerto Rico.

In 1962, the Puerto Rican government and the Economic and Social Council (ECOSO) set up a Nutrition Training Program for Latin America in Puerto Rico.

Since the mid-1960s, in an attempt to reduce the high number of unemployed, the EDA developed some training programs. For instance, in 1964, the Economic Opportunity Act for young people from disadvantaged groups was approved.

The Act set the Community Action Program to encourage communities to mobilise their resources to fight unemployment among young people.

That year, 1964, the Upward Bound Project, in collaboration with the Inter-American University of Puerto Rico, offered grants to poor young who wanted to follow university studies started.

The following year, 1965, the Public Welfare Division implemented a program to provide training in industrial and vocational arts for unemployed adults which resulted to be extremely successful.

The EDA also tried to reduce unemployment by encouraging the deeply neglected agrarian sector and, by 1970, public investment in agricultural development amounted to more than $150 million[xxv].

The Negative Consequences of the Operation Bootstrap

By the late 1960s, the Operation Bootstrap was running into problems. The Puerto Rican economy became increasingly dependent on United States' investments with some disastrous consequences.

One of them was the neglect of local business, such as Puerto Rican beer, which had been highly productive before industrial development began. The needlework industry, which was the single successful manufacturing activity prior to Operation Bootstrap's implementation, was also in decline.

The new protective labour laws and the consolidation of the minimum wage in the sector were also provoking a slowdown of jobs.

In addition, many branches of big American companies opened their doors leaving the small local businesses unable to compete and spreading American culture throughout the island.

Another problem was that Puerto Rico did not developed its own industrial system, but just became a centre for transforming American raw materials into goods and benefits, which would afterwards return to the mainland.

Operation Bootstrap also damaged the agricultural sector by focusing on industrial development. In 1940, Puerto Rico's farms produced around $70.5 million or 31% of the net income of the island. In 1969, by contrast, the farms produced $175.5 million but that figure represented only 5% of the island's net income. This neglect of the agrarian sector also resulted in a massive loss of jobs.

A further problem was the loss of a huge amount of money in revenue due to Puerto Rican tax exemption policy. An example of this is that, in 1969, none of the island's seven bigger banks were paying a cent in income taxes with the consequent loss of millions of dollars in revenue.

On the other hand, the plan attracted industrial not labour intensive businesses. Many of the Puerto Rican industries produced considerable benefits but did not generate many jobs. The situation worsened by the late 1960s and early 1970s when big petrochemical companies were established on the island. These companies produced, among others things, plastic, synthetic material and medicine, and utilised heavy machinery that needed only a few people to be operated.

At the same time, although between 1964 and 1967 the industrial development program was able to create some 30,000 new jobs, Puerto Rico's population growth continued and, by 1965, the unemployment rate was as high as 21%[xxvi].

The Extending of the Tax-Exempted Laws

In trying to resolve the problem, the EDA developed a number of ideas like the approval, in 1963, of another Industrial Incentive Act that and allowed a further ten-year period of income and property exemption for new industries. That meant that any industry established in 1974 would be tax-exempted until 1984.

A further provision, in 1970, reduced taxes by considering related corporation and partnerships as a single unit for tax revenue purposes.

In 1978, a new provision granted partial tax exemption for a period of twenty years with 90% exemption during the first 5 years, declining gradually to 55% in the last 5 years.

The EDA allocated money for improving the public services and the island's infrastructure like a 1967 program that allocated $69 million to finance expenditures in industrial and tourist facilities, new schools, new housing, land purchase and rural water supplies.

The Decline of the "Economic Miracle" of Puerto Rico

The EDA's efforts to sanitise Puerto Rican economy were fruitless and, by the 1970s, the success of Operation Bootstrap was over due to several reasons.

For instance, in 1968, the political dominance of the Popular Democratic Party had come to an end. From then on, a series of short-lived governments made instability the characteristic feature of Puerto Rican politics discouraging, in that way, American investment in the island. That same year, 1968, Puerto Rico's Minimum Wage Board enforced the minimum wage. By 1970, the island's wages were very close to those in the Southern States of the Union and around three times higher than in most Latin American countries.

As a result, many American enterprises moved to other undeveloped countries in Latin American, Asia and Africa where they could find a cheaper labour force.

The years 1971 and 1972 saw an economic recession on the mainland, which negatively affected a highly dependent Puerto Rican economy.

The recession also generated a wave of emigration in reverse. Between 1970 and 1974, thousands of Puerto Ricans returned to the island than left it, contributing to the unemployment problem.

The single industry which continued to generate benefits during great part of the 1970s was tourism. However, by the late 1970s, the Puerto Rican tourist industry's fate changed when it faced a crisis in having to compete with other popular destinations, such as Mexico, Disneyland and, after reductions in transatlantic tickets, Europe.

Overall, although infrastructure and welfare were greatly improved, the island's economy continued to stagnate. The Puerto Rican government public debt in 1950 had been $119 million, but by 1972 it had climbed to $2,555 million[xxvii]. By 1975, the average Puerto Rican family lived on an income just 59% of that of a mainland family.

By the late 1970s, the unemployment rate had climbed to over 20% and the agrarian sector had suffered a massive jobs losses.

Also, in 1973, President Richard Nixon decided to suspend the Federal Housing Program in Puerto Rico, causing a crisis in the construction sector with the consequent loss of jobs and the worsening of housing quality. By 1980, 40% of housing was still classified as inadequate and many people continued living in slums.

The situation was so desperate that the federal government was forced to increase aid to the island. From September 1974 to January 1975, the arrival of the Food Stamp Program, designed to grant economic aid to the poor, rescued Puerto Rican economy. By the late 1970s, around 71% of the island's population qualified for food stamps[xxviii] allocating around $1.7 billion.

> The United States was shocked when, in 1978, it became known that two-thirds of all families on the island qualified for food stamps. The federal government had not been aware of this level of poverty on the island. The industrial development has suffered some sever setbacks. Agricultural employment has dropped seriously in the past thirty years, and the increase in jobs through economic development has never been able to keep up with the increasing numbers entering the labour force[xxix].

Having realising the Operation Bootstrap's inability to resolve the long-term economic problems of the island, many Puerto Ricans decided to leave their country. The United States mainland, with its increasing Puerto Rican community, was the logical destination.

Chapter 7: Puerto Rican Migration to the Mainland

Before the Spanish-American War of 1898, Puerto Rican immigration to the United States was limited to a few intellectuals, a small number of upper class students and a handful of the more nationalist elements conspiring against Spanish rule. Once Puerto Rico became an American possession, only a few adventurous tried their luck in the new metropolis.

By the 1930s, the Great Depression and its consequent loss of jobs on the mainland, meant that Puerto Ricans refrained from leaving the island.

By the mid-1940s the United States had overcome its depression and emerged from World War II a superpower. The American economy was booming and with it the demand for labour. United States' businesses held Puerto Ricans in high esteem as they were hard workers and were willing to work for less money than Americans. Also, they were American citizens and did not need visas and work permits.

On the other hand, migration to the mainland was encouraged by the Puerto Rican government in order to control the island's overpopulation problem. As a result, from 1945 to 1960, over half a million Puerto Ricans left the island to become cheap labour in the United States and live in the worst slums on the mainland.

Traditionally, Puerto Rican immigrants were semi or unskilled workers, with little education (only 30% had finished high school), most of them were very young single men or divorced adults (around 80% of them were 25 years old or less) who settled in urban areas, mainly in New York City.

The New York Ricans

Since the early days of Puerto Rican migration to the mainland, New York City with its cosmopolitan mixture of cultures became the favourite destination of these poor migrants who believed that the "big apple" was the answer to their economic problems.

Steadily, however, the American dream was transformed into a nightmare. Puerto Ricans suddenly realised that they belonged to an ethnic minority with a different cultural and historical background. Furthermore, most Puerto Rican migrants proceeded from rural areas in Puerto Rico and having to adapt to a big, and at times cold city like New York, was a difficult task.

Puerto Ricans on the mainland also found themselves belonging to a religious minority and, unlike other emigrant groups, such as the Italians and the Irish, they neither brought clergy personalities with them nor built their own parishes which, could provide a sense of community for the newcomers.

Even the theoretically positive fact of being American citizens and not needing work and residence permits played a negative role because, often, Puerto Ricans were confused with other Hispanic groups.

As Puerto Rican individuals were not requested to hold a passport when travelling to the mainland, they could not prove their American citizenship. Therefore, they were often suspected of being illegal aliens with the consequent difficulties of finding and retaining a job.

Housing also represented a problem as most Puerto Ricans were extremely poor and had a larger number of children than the average American family, resulting in the impossibility of affording adequate housing.

In addition, the Puerto Rican community suffered a serious lack of political representation as a great sector of community was under the voting age and a reduced number of eligible voters were, in fact, registered to vote.

The Educative Challenge of the New York Ricans

When arriving in New York, Puerto Rican children found themselves having to study in a language other than their mother tongue and being taught by teachers who could not understand them. The result was a high number of drop-outs, which deeply influenced the economic situation of the Puerto Rican community and contributed to the fact that with the entrance of the 1970s decades, around one-third of Puerto Ricans in the mainland were living in poverty.

Puerto Rican low educational performance also influenced in the growing rate of drug addiction among the community's youth. In 1969, the Hispanic association for a Drug Free Society was founded to try to keep Hispanic youngsters away from drugs.

In trying to offer an answer to the problem of the low educational attainment of Puerto Ricans, many American officials named money as the solution. However, this argument was ruled out, as New York State was already the second highest spending state in the nation on school expenditure.

Another argument blamed Hispanic students and their parents for their community's low performance.

The real reasons for Puerto Ricans' low achievements in education differed from the official arguments. One reason was that many Puerto Rican young were forced to leave school and join the labour market in order to contribute to the family's income. Also, Hispanic students had little confidence that there would be a significant pay-off for their investment of time, as the difference in salaries between Anglo-Saxon Americans and Hispanics increased at higher levels of schooling.

Some attempts to reduce this high drop-out rate were made. For instance, in 1948, a report of the Association of Assistant superintendents emphasised the need to use bilingual auxiliary teachers for the Spanish-speaking children.

In 1965, there were around 2,000 auxiliaries in elementary schools but it was not enough to resolve the problem, as most of them could not speak Spanish[xxx].

In 1968 the Bilingual Education Act was approved by Congress in an attempt for reversing the poor level of performance of the Hispanic students. During the late 1960s and early 1970s, different courses in Puerto Rican culture and history were introduced in the New York universities while in 1972, the Puerto Rican community sued the New York City Board of Education in an attempt to force New York City's school to apply the bilingual program, as stipulated in the 1968 Bilingual Act to all the students entitled to it[xxxi].

Nevertheless, all these efforts were unsuccessful and, by 1972, although 30% of the New York City's student population were of Hispanic origin (the majority Puerto Ricans), Hispanic teachers accounted for just 2% of New York educational staff.

Two years after its introduction, the Bilingual Act was not providing visible results. In 1970, only 60% of those students legally entitled to it were receiving some kind of bilingual education and only half of these 60% were offered a fully bilingual education which contributed to a drop-out rate of almost 70%.

The Support of the Latin Population

Throughout the years, Puerto Ricans have founded different organisations that addressed the numerous problems that their community faced in New York City.

In 1948, the Puerto Rican government opened an office of the Commonwealth of Puerto Rico to help newcomers to overcome cultural barriers while the Migration Division of the Puerto Rico Department of Labour in New York established a program to raise the awareness of migrants about living conditions in the city.

In the mid-1950s, a group of the young educated and intellectuals founded the Puerto Rican Forum.

In 1961, with the aim of providing inspiration and encouraging further education and guidance among the Puerto Rican youth, the Forum established "Aspira" (Be Inspired).

Four years later, in 1965, the Forum established a second organisation, the Puerto Rican Community Development Project, to help Puerto Ricans develop a sense of community and identity. That same year, the Puerto Rican Family Institute opened its doors to provide social services to the community.

In the earlier-1960s, a group of students, the Young Lords, became active in universities.

The Young Lords' aim was to defend the rights of Puerto Rican students in the campuses but they also founded a newspaper, Pa'lante (Forward). By the late 1960s, the Lords changed their name and became the Puerto Rican Revolutionary Workers Association.

From then on, the association, which at the start had been politically focused, centred on social issues organising, among others, a program of free breakfast for Puerto Rican children and a clothing distribution program among the Puerto Rican community.

Also, in 1972, the Puerto Rican Legal Defence and Education Fund began to offer free legal advice to the Hispanic community.

The establishment of these associations resulted in the appearance, by the 1970s, of a sense of identity and pride of being Puerto Ricans among the Puerto Rican community.

The Decades of the 1970s and the 1980s in New York

The 1970s arrived bringing some problems that caused a tremendous blow to the Puerto Rican community in New York.

One of these events was the economic recession experienced by the United States in 1971 and 1972, which led to a substantial increase in the unemployment rate among Puerto Ricans.

From 1970 to 1980, New York became an international financial and business centre, resulting in the loss of almost 500,000 jobs in the manufacturing sector[xxxii].

This decline of manufacturing jobs caused a worsening of the economic situation of Puerto Ricans in New York who were broadly represented in this sector.

As a result, by 1980, Puerto Ricans were the poorest sector of New York society with over 40% of Puerto Rican families in the city receiving public welfare[xxxiii].

At the same time, the housing problem was becoming more preoccupying. Most Puerto Ricans lived in the South Bronx, East Harlem (Spanish Harlem), and a small number of them in Manhattan, Queens and Staten Island. From 1970 to 1980, the so-called "Burning of the Bronx" took place, resulting in the loss of 57% of Puerto Rican housing and the dispersal of the community.

Additionally, during that decade, Manhattan vastly extended and big buildings were taken over the Barrios with the further loss of Puerto Rican's housing.

In 1978, the South Bronx Development Organisation was set up to study the problem of housing in the Bronx.

However, no improvement occurred and although, by 1980, the authorities of New York City allocated $7 million a year to demolish damaged buildings in the Bronx nothing was done to reallocate the families who lost their houses[xxxiv].

Finding it impossible to deal with the increasingly hostile situation in New York, many Puerto Ricans resolved to migrate to other United States cities. The 1980 United States Census showed that Puerto Ricans had established themselves in great number in other cities apart from New York, such as New Jersey, Chicago, Philadelphia, Boston, San Francisco, Los Angeles and Miami.

Some other New York Ricans decided that the solution stood in returning to Puerto Rico and by 1977, around half of a million of Puerto Ricans had returned to their island.

This wave of migration in reverse brought with it several problems as the returned migrants found it difficult to adapt to life on the island while being unable to find a job as the rate of unemployment on the island was higher than on the United States' mainland.

Agrarian Migrants

Since the 1920s, several American companies reached agreements with the Puerto Rican government for the importation of Puerto Rican cheap labour.

In January 1949, an agreement between Puerto Rico's Secretary of Labour and the National Director of the Bureau of Employment Security was signed to implement a program through which Puerto Rican migrants were provided as farm workers to several states, such as Pennsylvania, Connecticut and mainly New Jersey.

The Puerto Rican workers were highly desired by the American farms as they represented cheap labour and did not require resident and work permits. Almost 5,000 seasonal migrants joined the program in its first year and, by 1970, around 50,000 Puerto Ricans were working for periods of six to nine months in farms in Connecticut, New Jersey and Massachusetts.

From the mid-1970s onwards, the decline in the number of Puerto Rican farm workers on United States farms was significant as, working under dreadful health conditions and without the protection of the Minimum Wage Law, Puerto Ricans learnt to form associations in order to defend their rights.

In 1973, the first union of agrarian workers, La Asociación de Trabajadores Agrícolas (ATA) was established in New Jersey. In the summer of 1979, the Farm Workers Support Committee was organised to support Puerto Rican farm workers regarding social, political and human rights issues in New Jersey. By the mid-1970s, the unions began legal action against employers for breaking contracts without compensation, exploitation of employees and other labour disputes.

This seasonal migration, nevertheless, did not resolve the problem of unemployment on the island as these migrants returned to spend the rest of the year in Puerto Rico. Furthermore, the wages that they had brought from the mainland did not last long and soon, they were forced to request federal aid to survive the rest of the season.

Chapter 8: The Commonwealth of Puerto Rico

Local politics in Puerto Rico were characterised by the absolute dominance of the Popular Democratic Party or Partido Popular Democrático (PPD) with its leader, Luis Muñoz Marín, as the most charismatic Puerto Rican political figure.

The Popular Democratic Party (PPD), which was founded in 1932, would stay in power from 1940 to 1968. None of the other important local parties of that period, including the conservative Republican Party, renamed the Statehood Party in 1948; the Puerto Rican Independentist Party (PIP), founded in 1946; and the Nationalist Party[xxxv], founded in 1922, offered the slightest resistance.

During the 1940s, Muñoz and the "populares" realised that the island's relationship with the United States was in need of some modifications and, with that objective in mind they began to pressure Washington for more autonomy.

In early 1945, Muñoz requested a referendum from Congress on Puerto Rico's status. The result was that, in October 1945, President Harry S. Truman proposed a plebiscite, refused by Congress, in which Puerto Ricans would choose whether they wanted independence, statehood, colony status or to become a more self-governed territory.

Three years later, in 1948, Muñoz pressed Congress again demanding that Puerto Rico be allowed to have its own Constitution. Furthermore, on January 2, 1949 Muñoz Marín became the first elected Governor in the history of the Caribbean Island after the Crawford-Butler Act, known as the Elective Governor Act, had been approved by Congress two years earlier, in 1947[xxxvi].

Local Politics, PPD leadership and the Commonwealth of Puerto Rico

The political pressures of the PPD in Puerto Rico and its Resident Commissioner in Washington, Fernos Isern, obtained that, in July 1950, the U.S. Congress called for a convention to meet from September 1951 to February 1952 in order to draft a Constitution for Puerto Rico.

Some innovative measures were introduced like the Bill converted Puerto Rico into an Estado Libre Asociado or Commonwealth of Puerto Rico[xxxvii]. It also granted the island a Bill of Rights, its own Constitution, and fiscal and cultural autonomy while retaining the advantages of American citizenship and a common market that facilitated both, emigration to the mainland, and United States investment.

The bill also had its disadvantages, such as the fact that the United States retained absolute power over Puerto Rico's foreign relations and trade. Congress could also repeal any measure approved by the Puerto Rican legislature, including amendments to the island's Constitution.

In March 1952, the final draft of the Puerto Rican Constitution was presented to the people of Puerto Rico for their acceptance, receiving almost 70% of votes[xxxviii]. Eventually, Public Law 600, official name of the Constitutional Bill, was signed by President Truman on July 3, 1952 and came into effect the 25th of July 1952, just 54 years after Americans had landed in Puerto Rico.

Advocates of statehood were not happy with the result as they thought that, although Commonwealth did not grant self-government, it was the first step to independence. Independence supporters were not impressed either with the political change, as they believed that the Commonwealth only extended Puerto Rico's colonial status.

The major shortcoming of the Commonwealth lies in the fact that virtually no aspect of local life is free of the superior federal authority. Federal control of foreign policy does not necessarily interfere with local autonomy. However, the United States also decides who may enter in Puerto Rico, where Puerto Ricans may go, and whether Puerto Ricans will fight in foreign wars. Banking, currency and the mail are under federal jurisdiction, as are all laws concerning bankruptcy, naturalisation and citizenship... Puerto Ricans still have no voice in their tariffs, trade arrangements and they must still transport their goods in American ships. The United States retains unlimited power to expropriate Puerto Rican lands and property. The drastic limits on insular autonomy have led many Puerto Ricans to ridicule the "compact" as nothing more than a cosmetic device to hide American sovereignty on the island[xxxix].

Chapter 9: Local Politics

By the late 1950s, it was evident, even for Muñoz and the Popular Party that the compact had barely changed the political status of Puerto Rico and that Congress was still retaining too much power.

Once more, Puerto Rican government pressed Washington for more autonomy. In September 1959, Resident Commissioner, Fernós Isern and Congressman James Murray introduced the Fernós-Murray Bill to Congress. The bill, which was rejected by Congress, requested among other things, more autonomy for the island and the right of Puerto Rico to fix its own tariffs.

Another PPD attempt to change the situation took place in April 1963. After an exchange of letters between the Puerto Rican governor, Muñoz Marín and the American President, John F. Kennedy, the PPD called for the establishment of a 12-month United States-Puerto Rico Commission. The Commission would study a new compact to grant Puerto Ricans, among other things, sovereignty over the island and the right to participate in international organisations[xl].

The Bill, Public Law 88-271, was signed by President Lyndon B. Johnson in February 1964 and a 13-member commission, six Puerto Ricans and seven Americans, met from June 1964 to August 1966[xli].

During the course of those two years, the commission turned down basically all of Muñoz's demands. Its single conclusion was that a referendum on the status of Puerto Rico should be held where the island's inhabitants would be asked whether they wanted a Commonwealth, statehood or independence.

The plebiscite took place on June 23, 1967, with little more than 60% of Puerto Rican voters supporting a Commonwealth, 38% voting for statehood and just 0.6% for independence[xlii].

The Arrival of the New Progressive Party

In 1968, the PPD's political hegemony ended when, four years after Muñoz's retirement from politics, a new party pro-statehood party, the New Progressive Party (NPP), won the General Elections. NPP's leader, Luis Ferré, continued Muñoz's line of pressing Washington for some modifications to the United States-Puerto Rico relationship.

Puerto Rican pressure had some results. For instance, in 1970, the Puerto Rican Resident Commissioner was granted the right to vote in the House.

At the same time, Governor Ferré requested Congress to allow Puerto Ricans to vote in the presidential elections. Consequently, in July 1970, President Richard Nixon allowed the formation of an Ad Hoc Committee to discuss this possibility. In August 1971, the mentioned committee recommended that Puerto Ricans should be granted the right to vote to elect the United States President and Vice-president. The Committee's recommendations were finally ignored by Congress.

Four years later, in 1975, Puerto Rican Resident Commissioner, Jaime Benítez, introduced another bill in Congress to allow Puerto Rico to fix its own tariffs on imports and exports and implement its own immigration laws.

The bill also called for the participation of Puerto Rico in international organisations and its representation in the United States Senate. However, in August 1976, President Gerald Ford vetoed it and instead, in January 1977, he introduced a bill calling for statehood, only to find Congress rejecting it[xliii].

During the Jimmy Carter administration, January 1977-1981, Puerto Rican politicians obtained a few small victories. For instance, in early 1977, a new Ad Hoc Group proposed that Puerto Rico's English name should be changed from the Commonwealth of Puerto Rico to its Spanish name Free Associated State and recommended a Puerto Rican representative in each house. Both recommendations were granted by Congress.

Also, in July 1978, President Carter spoke about the holding of a referendum on four possible options. The first option was independence, the second statehood, the third Commonwealth and, for the first time, President Carter spoke about a fourth option, very much favoured by the people of Puerto Rico, a modified Commonwealth. The following year, in 1979, Carter ordered the Kreeps Report, the first study on the social and economic problems of the island.

The Decade of the 1980s in Puerto Rico

Any hope of obtaining more self-government vanished when President Ronald Reagan and his successor, President George Bush Sr., implemented a pro-statehood policy towards Puerto Rico.

Both Presidents delivered numerous speeches calling for Puerto Rico's entrance in the Union. Additionally, President Bush Sr. visited the island on several occasions during his presidency in order to gain local support for his pro-statehood policy.

For several reasons, United States Congress had never seriously considered the possibility of Puerto Rico becoming part of the Union.

One of the reasons for this rejection was that the Caribbean Island was seen as far too poor to become a State while another reason for congressional refusal of statehood status was political power. Puerto Rico with its large population would ensure more voting strength in the United States' House of Representatives than 20 existing states of the Union.

In addition, if Puerto Rico in the majority voted Democrat, the Republicans would refuse statehood and if the island voted Republican, the Democrats would refuse it entrance to the Union.

Many Americans did not consider Puerto Rico ready to become a state as they regarded its people as culturally inferior and unwilling to embrace the American culture and values. This fact has been evident by Puerto Ricans constant rejection of the English language.

Independence, on the contrary, was an option supported only by a small group of Puerto Ricans as most of the islanders viewed it as economic suicide as it could cut off United States' investment and federal aid on which the island was heavily dependent.

Besides, the United States Congress was not ready either to grant a major degree of self-government, fearing that the many American business interests on the island could be affected. There was also the paternalistic belief that Puerto Ricans, like most Latin Americans, were not prepared for self-government.

This American attitude created consternation and criticism among that part of the international community that regarded United States' rule in Puerto Rico as imperialistic.

Chapter 10: Puerto Rico and the International Community.

Since the founding of the United Nations (UN) in 1945, the United States had advocated for the end of colonialism.

That year of 1945 the United Nations' General Assembly approved one of its first chapters, the UN Chapter 73. The Chapter requested UN members with territorial dependencies to present a list of their protectorates and to keep the Committee on Information from Non-Self-Governing Territories, set in 1947, informed about the political, economic and social conditions in those territories. The Committee would examine the situation of, among others, the territories dependent on the United States like Puerto Rico.

In the meantime, many countries found increasingly ironic that the United States pressed for decolonization at the same time that kept Puerto Rico in a rather ambiguous political status.

The Relation between the United States and the United Nations

In November 1953 the General Assembly presented Resolution 742 (VIII), which explained that, in order to be considered self-governed, a country had to possess full international responsibility, be eligible for membership of the United Nations, conduct its own international relations, provide its own national defence, possess total autonomy in social, economic and cultural issues and have legislative representation[xliv].

Although by then the inhabitants of Puerto Rico had chosen the implementation of the Commonwealth status through referendum, the island did not fulfil some of the UN's basic requisites to be considered a self-governed country. The island could not participate in international bodies, it could not provide its own defence and it did not have representation in the U.S. Congress and Senate.

The same day that Resolution 742 was passed, November 27, 1953, the United Nations General Assembly, at the United States request, passed its Resolution 748 (VIII). This Resolution considered that Puerto Rico had acquired an independent constitutional status and recommended the removal of the Caribbean island from the list of non-self-governing countries.

Also, on December 14, 1960, the General Assembly passed its Resolution 1514. This Resolution explained that a territory could be considered self-governed when it was an independent state, it had freely associated with an independent state on the basis of total equality or it had freely decided to integrate with an independent state. This Resolution also declared that "an associated territory should have the right to determinate its internal constitution without outside interference"[xlv]. Although Puerto Rico had freely expressed its wish for association with the United States, the island's Constitution needed the approval of the U.S. Congress and Puerto Ricans could not amendment it without previously consulting and gaining endorsement from the U.S. Congress and President.

The Debate on Puerto Rico in the United Nations during the 1960s and 1970s

During the 1960s and beyond, the United Nations began to recognise the exceptional nature of Puerto Rico's political status. By then, many countries that had previously been colonies, became independent and joined the United Nations. This event considerably increased the number of United Nations, members who were very sensitive to colonial policies.

Cuba also started a campaign seeking independence for Puerto Rico independence. In 1965, and again in 1972, the Cuban government unsuccessfully demanded a debate on the status of Puerto Rico in the General Assembly.

In 1973, Cuba presented its demands again and, on that occasion, the Assembly granted them. As a result, from 1973 to 1977, the Decolonization Committee, set up by the General Assembly in 1961, conducted a study on the Puerto Rican question.

In 1977, the Committee concluded that Puerto Rico's status was that of a colony and demanded an end to American dominance over the island.

The following year, 1978, the Committee approved a resolution requesting that the United Nations resolutions on decolonization should be respected by all countries without exceptions.

The Decade of the 1980s in the United Nations

The decade of the 1980s started with the United Nations declaring that colonization was against the very own nature of the organisation.

Therefore, in 1981 and 1982, the Committee on Decolonization recommended that the United States-Puerto Rico relationship be discussed in the General Assembly.

These recommendations were very significant as they illustrated the increasing willingness of many United Nations' members to challenge the United States' official stand on Puerto Rico.

This was the first time since Puerto Rico's removal from the non-self-governing territories list in 1953, that recommendations for a debate on the island's political status were suggested.

Although a general feeling of anti-colonialism existed among United Nations' members, the United States managed to force the General Assembly to reject these recommendations.

Besides the United Nations, during the decades of the 1970s and 1980s, some other international organisations also accused the United States of conducting a colonial policy towards Puerto Rico as the Conference of Latin American Political Parties (COPPAL) that called for Puerto Rico's independence.

Also, in 1982, the Socialist International published a statement in which defended the right of the Puerto Ricans to self-government.

The Debate on the Political Status of Puerto Rico Nowadays

In June 2011 Cuba, with the backing of Venezuela, Bolivia, Nicaragua and Ecuador, presented a new project of resolution to grant Puerto Rico the freedom to determinate what kind of relationship the country wishes to maintain with the United States.

The Cuban proposal came just a few days after the White House published a report recommending a referendum in Puerto Rico to allow its inhabitants to decide whether or not they wanted to become a state of the Union or preferred to continue its commonwealth status.

The report of the White House was highly transcendental being this the first time that Washington seriously considered the possibility of granting the status of State to Puerto Rico.

At the moment and according to all statistics, except a minority that wishes Independence, Puerto Ricans find themselves divided between continuing with its current status and becoming a State.

The common sense of modern times invites to introduce numerous modifications in the current status, including more representation of Puerto Rico in Washington and a higher degree of freedom at the moment of reaching trade and commercial agreement with third countries that could convert Puerto Rico into a truly Commonwealth while keeping international complaints at bay.

The international debate on the political status of Puerto Rico that started more than one century ago, seems to prolong in time.

Chapter 11: Conclusion

It is hard to believe that a small Caribbean island is still the focus of numerous debates and headaches at the heart of the most powerful country in the world, the United States. The United States granted Puerto Ricans a Constitution and American citizenship and transformed the island into a supposedly Free Associated State. However, Puerto Rico can still being regard as a colony as Puerto Ricans are not allowed to approve any law without the United States' consent; neither can they manage their international relations or immigration police.

Nowadays, the United States' Congress is still unable to decide whether or not to grant statehood to the island and this in spite the fact that in 2012 for the first time, Puerto Ricans shown themselves willing to become the State 51 of the Union through no official referendum. Puerto Rico's poverty is a source of concern for many Americans who believe that if it were to become a state, Puerto Rico could be an economic burden to the United States.

In addition, many Americans have the opinion that the island is far "too Spanish" to join the Union while their Spanish inheritance and language is something that the Puerto Ricans are not willing to sacrifice for the sake of statehood.

The prospect of independence also seems to be problematic because it is seen as hugely negative to American interests on the island while Puerto Ricans contemplate that it would be tantamount to economic suicide.

With regard to Commonwealth status, American opinion on the mainland is that the United States has been extremely generous to Puerto Rico and that the island is free to change its relationship with the United States at any time.

American public opinion ignores the fact that Puerto Ricans have no power to modify the Commonwealth compact, nor can they introduce any law without the consent of the United States Congress.

This was shown in 1991 when the Puerto Rican legislature declared Spanish as the only official language of the island, only to have the decision repealed by the United States Congress two years later.

On the other hand, American Congress has continuously disregarded the island's demands to implement modifications to the Commonwealth contract.

This fact became evident when, in June 1991, and again in 1998, the United States Congress ignored the results of two more popular plebiscites held on Puerto Rico's status.

Then, although most Puerto Ricans favoured maintaining ties with the United States, they demanded some changes to the Commonwealth agreement that would allow them to organise their economic, social and political life in accordance with their own ideas of liberty, security and happiness, and not American ones

These demands have also been voiced by part of the international community who, several times, has requested the United Nation General Assembly to look into the Puerto Rican question.

It cannot be denied that, in the years of American presence, Puerto Rican education system has been developed and Puerto Rico enjoys one of the most advanced and democratic life styles in Latin America.

Also, from 1941 onwards, government efforts to develop Puerto Rico's economy impressively transformed the island from an agrarian into an industrial society while improving its infrastructure and welfare conditions.

Nevertheless, Puerto Rico's economy has become increasingly integrated with and consequently dependent on the American one. Unlike the United States and European economies, which are focused on mass production of goods with a solid industrial base, Puerto Rico was, and still is, a distributing entity. The island is limited to transforming the mainland's raw materials into goods, which then are sold back to the United States.

The agricultural sector had been massively affected by industralization. From 1950 to 1983, the production of sugar, the main agrarian resource of the island, sugar, declined by almost 90% while the other two more important crops in Puerto Rico's agriculture, coffee and tobacco, basically vanished.

Once the initial boom created by the development program was swept away, the cruel reality showed through again. The attempt at industrial development did not success in finding a long-term solution to the island's problems. By 1980, over 62% of Puerto Ricans lived below the national poverty line while the unemployment rate climbed to almost 30%, three times more than the mainland; and 60% of families were dependent on federal aid and the external debt of the country jumped to $8.1 billion[xlvi].

At the same time, the United States implemented the Caribbean Basin Initiative (CBI) which called for free trade between the United States and the whole Caribbean area cutting off the advantages that Puerto Rico had enjoyed over the rest of the region.

Puerto Rico had based its economic survival on American charity and by 1984, Puerto Rico received $4 billion in Food Stamps and 70% of the island's population qualified for federal aid.

At the same time, the official unemployment figure reached 20% but, with a great number of the employed working only a few hours a week, the unofficial unemployment rate climbed to around 40%[xlvii].

In the early 1970s, Puerto Rico was held up as a showcase of economic development, as a shining example of how political stability, democracy, and open-market economic policies lead to economic growth. This image has been tarnished by the island's disappointing and painful social and economic experiences of the last thirty years[xlviii].

Throughout the years, the numerous attempts made by the Puerto Rican government to control one of the biggest problems of the island, its overpopulation had not been very successful either. Puerto Rico recurred to emigration as a way to relief the island of its excess of labour.

As a result, thousands of Puerto Ricans were encouraged by their government to migrate to the mainland.

Once there, these migrants realised that their economic situation was not about to change substantially and that they had to face problems of adapting to a foreign culture and language, as well as racial discrimination.

Although the 1980s and 1990s saw a significant increase of Puerto Ricans in semi professional and technical occupations, unemployment levels were still much higher than the United States average. Additionally, school drop-outs remained a preoccupying issue while many families were still living under the poverty level and in inadequate housing.

The different problems found for the Puerto Rican community in the mainland, provoked a wave of migration in reverse, especially during the 1970s, that worsened the problem of overpopulation in the island.

Also, during that decade the island's population continued growing at an unstoppable pace and it was only during the 1980s that Puerto Rico's high birth rate began to come under control. The higher educational attainment of the population began to influence the number of children born on the island. As a result, between 1980 and 1990, Puerto Rico's population increased by little more than 300,000 people reaching the figure of 3,522,000 individuals[xlix].

Overall, in the 21st century, Puerto Rico continues to be a small, improvised, overpopulated island, economically dependent on the metropolis for its very subsistence. The industrial development that took place on the island during the 1940s, 1950s and 1960s, although successful, was not enough to sanitise Puerto Rican economy. By the 1990s, the economic picture of the island was desolate. In 1990, Puerto Rican income per capita was $5,200 compared with $14,948 in the United States while the island's external debt amounted to over $8,400 billion[i].

In 1995, the U.S. Congress struck a "coup de grace" in the Puerto Rican economy by abolishing the tax exemption period which Puerto Rican-based industries had long enjoyed.

Operation Bootstrap, which had converted the island into a tax free paradise, came to an end and with it great part of the foreign investment in Puerto Rico. Social conditions were also appealing and, by the 1990s, 57% of the island's families were living in poverty[li].

Puerto Rican culture was also bombarded through American investments, as well as radio and television stations while the constant migration to the mainland resulted in a dispersal of the island's population. As a result, by the year 2000, there were 3.8 million people living in Puerto Rico and almost another 3 million Puerto Ricans on the mainland. In other words, by that year, almost 50% of Puerto Ricans were living outside the island.

This population dispersal brought with it same social problems, such as the fact that many Puerto Ricans on the island saw those on the mainland as far too "Americanise". On the contrary, Puerto Ricans on the mainland regarded those in Puerto Rico as elitist with no idea about the problems that their fellow Puerto Ricans faced outside their country. Also, the generation of Puerto Ricans born on the mainland found difficult to identify themselves with their parent's island.

After more than a century of American presence, although Commonwealth status has contributed to the development of a democratic system characterised by political stability and the elimination of corruption at high levels, Puerto Rico enjoys less rights than during the last months of Spanish rule when the Puerto Rican Chapter of Autonomy was implemented.

While the political status continues to cause heated arguments on the island and headaches on the mainland, Puerto Rico's future remains a mystery that only the United States can resolve. Perhaps, one day the United States will finally listen to Puerto Rican claims for more autonomy and convert Puerto Rico into a true Free Associated State, relieving this small Caribbean island of the stigma of being the oldest colony in the world.

STATISTICS

TABLE 1

NUMBER OF INHABITANTS IN PUERTO RICO- 1910 TO 1990[lii]

Year	Total Inhabitants
1910	1,118,000
1920	1,299,809
1930	1,543,913
1940	1,869,255
1950	2,210,000
1960	2,349,544
1970	2,712,033
1980	3,196,500
1990	3,522,037

TABLE 2

BIRTH AND DEATH RATES AND LIFE EXPECTANCY

IN PUERTO RICO-1940 TO 1980[liii]

Year	1940	1950	1960	1970	1980
Birth Rate (Thousand Inhabitants)	38.5	38.5	32.2	24.8	23.8
Death Rate (Thousand Inhabitants)	18.4	9.9	6.7	6.7	6.6
Life Expectancy (In Years)	46	60	69	72	73

TABLE 3

PUERTO RICANS BORN OUTSIDE PUERTO RICO, 1910-1970[liv]

Year	Outside Puerto Rico (In Thousands)	Born in the U.S.A. (%)
1910	14,266	15
1920	10,895	25
1930	9,378	30
1940	13,117	55
1950	22,678	60
1960	64,279	80
1970	187,229	85

TABLE 4

EMPLOYMENT IN MANUFACTURING BY INDUSTRY GROUP
SELECTED YEARS[iv]

Industry	1949	1958	1967	1977	1982
Food products	23,243	17,082	21,187	21,407	18, 621
Tobacco products	7, 116	4,509	6,899	3,670	NA
Apparel	10,850	17,998	34,474	35,294	31,876
Furniture/wood	2,215	3,327	4,505	3,206	2,798
Chemicals Products	1,268	1,483	2,885	15,732	17,225
Metal products	310	2,433	4,369	6,221	4,236
Textile products	NA	4,444	5,753	6,001	2,840
Printing/ publishing	1,459	1,516	2,482	4,037	2,861
Leather products	911	2,620	10,312	6,165	6,019
Rubber/plastic products	NA	1,022	2,235	5,961	4,496
Transportation	NA	NA	517	1,127	909
Paper products	294	635	1,287	1,459	1,469
Petroleum/coal	NA	NA	1,709	2,462	NA
Instruments	NA	NA	517	1,127	909
Machinery	617	3,752	9,726	18,856	28,404
Miscellaneous	2,389	3,964	3,438	3,487	3,373
Stone, clay & glass	2,562	4,131	6,211	4,987	4,390
TOTAL	55,137	71,188	121,537	146,861	143,218

TABLE 5

ECONOMIC INDICATORS- 1940 TO 1984 (In constant 1954 prices)[lvi]

	REAL GNP	
Year	Total (Million $)	Per Capita (U.S. Dollars)
1940	499	121
1952	925	415
1955	1,139	510
1960	1,473	630
1965	2,099	817
1968	2,455	927
1970	2,901	1,070
1975	3,374	1,158
1977	3,623	1,189
1980	4,077	1,281
1982	3,977	1,222
1984	4,083	1,249

The figures correspondent to the year 1975 reflected how the economic recession that took place on United States mainland, in the earlier 1970s, affected Puerto Rico. A second economic recession swept the United States in 1981 and 1982, and it had a profound impact on Puerto Rico's economy and was reflected in the slowdown of Puerto Rico's Gross National Product and income per capita in 1982 and 1983.

BIBLIOGRAPHY

Books

• Albizú Campos, P., *La Coinciencia Nacional Puertorriqueña* (Ciudad de Méjico/Madrid/Buenos Aires: Siglo Veintiuno Editores, S.A., 1972).

• Bhana, S., *The United States and the Development of the Puerto Rican Status Question, 1936-1968* (Lawrence: The University Press of Kansas, 1975).Bonilla Santiago, G., *Organising Puerto Rican Migrant Farmworkers: The Experience of Puerto Ricans in New Jersey* (New York: P. Land, 1988).

• Burma, J., *Spanish-Speaking Groups in the United States,* (Durham: Duke University Press, 1954).

• Carroll, H. K., *Report on the Island of Puerto Rico,* (New York: Arno Press, 1975).

• Chase, S., *"Operation Bootstrap" in Puerto Rico: Report of Progress,* (Washington D.C.: The National Planning Association Business Committee on National Policy) (Sept. 1951, Vol.75).

• Crampsey, R.A., *Puerto Rico,* (Newton/Abbot: David and Charles Publishers, 1973).

- Lewis, G., *Puerto Rico: Freedom and Power in the Caribbean*, (New York/London: Monthly Review Press, 1963).

- Curet, E., *Puerto Rico: Development by Integration to the U.S.* /Río Piedras: Editorial Cultural, 1986).

- _____, *El Desarrollo Económico de Puerto Rico* (San Juan de Puerto Rico: Management Aid Centre, Inc., 1976).

- Duffy Burnett, C., and Marshall, B., *Foreign in a Domestic Sense: Puerto Rico, American Expansion and the Constitution*, (Durham: Duke University Press, 1969).

- Falk, P.S., *The Political Status of Puerto Rico*, (Lexington/Toronto: Lexington Books, 1986).

- Fernández, R., *The Disenchanted Island: Puerto Rico and the United States in the Twentieth Century*, (New York/Westport/Connecticut/London: Praeger Publishers, 1987).

- Figueroa, L., *Breve Historia de Puerto Rico, Vol.II*, (Río Piedras: Editorial Edil, Inc., 1979).

- Fitzpatrick, J.P., *Puerto Rican Americans: The Meaning of Migration to the Mainland, 2nd Ed.* (New Jersey: J.P. Prentice-Hall Inc., 1987).

- Friedrich, C.L., *Puerto Rico: Middle Road to Freedom* (New York: Rinehart and company, Inc., 1959).

• García, F.C., *Latinos and the Political System,* (Notre Dame: University of Notre Dame Press, 1988).

• García Martínez, A.L., *Idioma y Política: El Papel Desempeñado por los Idiomas Español e Inglés en la Relación Política Puerto Rico-Estados Unidos,* (San Juan: Editorial Cordillera, 1976).

• García Passalacqua, J.M., *Puerto Rico: Equality and Freedom at Issue,* (New York/Philadelphia/Toronto/Hong Kong/Tokyo/Eastbourne/Sydney: Praeger Publishers, 1984).

• Garza, C., *Puerto Ricans in the United States: The Struggle for Freedom,* (New York: Pathfinder Press, 1977).

• Golding, M.J., *A Short History of Puerto Rico,* (New York: Mentor Books, 1973).

• Gould, L.J., *La Ley Foraker: Raíces de la Política Colonial de los Estados Unidos* (San Juan de Puerto Rico: Universidad de Puerto Rico, 1969).

• Hanson, E.P., *Puerto Rico: Land of Wonders,* (New York: Alfred A. Knopf, 1960).

• Hibben, T. and Pico, R., *Industrial development of Puerto Rico and the Virgin Island of the United States* (San Juan: Caribbean Commission, 1948).

- Holbilk, K.and Swan, P.L., *Industrialisation and Employment in Puerto Rico, 1950-1972* (Austin: The University of Texas, 1975).

- Johnson, R.A., *Puerto Rico: Commonwealth or Colony?* (New York: Praeger Publishers, 1980).

- López Tamés, R., *El Estado Libre Asociado de Puerto Rico,* (Oviedo: Instituto de Estudios Jurídicos, 1970).

- López, A. and Petras, J., *Puerto Rico and Puerto Ricans: Studies in History and Society,* (New York/London/ Sydney/Toronto: Schenkman Publishing Company, 1974).

- Magruder, C., *Report on the Commonwealth Status of Puerto Rico,* (Pittsburgh: University of Pittsburgh Press, 1953).

- Maldonado, A.W., *Teodoro Moscoso and Puerto Rico's Operation Bootstrap* (Orlandon/Miami/Jacksonville/ Boca Ratón: University Press of Florida, 1997).

- Maldonado Denis, M., *Puerto Rico: Una Interpretación Histórico-Social,* (Madrid/Ciudad de Méjico/Buenos Aires: Siglo Veintiuno Editores, 1969).

- _____, *Puerto Rico y los Estados Unidos: Emigración y Colonialismo, Un Análysis Sociohistórico de la Emigración Puertorriquena,* (Ciudad de Méjico: Siglo Veintiuno Editores, 1976).

- Mathews, T., *Puerto Rican Politics and the New Deal,* (Gainesville: University of Florida Press, 1960).

- Montalvo Barbot, A., *Political Conflict and Constitutional Change in Puerto Rico, 1898-1952,* (Lanham: The University Press of America, Inc., 1997).

- Morales, J., *Puerto Rican Poverty and Migration: We Just Had to Try Elsewhere,* (New York/ Westport/London: Praeger Publishers, 1986).

- Morales Carrión, A., *Puerto Rico: A Political and Cultural History,* (New York: W.W. Norton and Company, Inc., 1983).

- Morales Otero, P. *Comentarios Alrededor del Desarrollo Político de Puerto Rico,* (San Juan: Biblioteca de Autores Puertorriqueños, 1976).

- _____, *Nuestros Problemas, 2nd Ed.* (San Juan de Puerto Rico: Biblioteca de Autores Puertorriqueños, 1945).

- Morales Yordán, J., *Desarrollo Político y Pobreza,* (San Juan: Editorial Cordillera, Inc., 1971).

- Morris, N., *Puerto Rico: Culture, Politics and Identity,* (Westport: Praeger Publishers, 1995).

- Nieves Falcón, L., *Diagnóstico de Puerto Rico,* (Río Piedras: Editorial Edil, Inc., 1972).

- Pagan, B., *Puerto Rico: The Next State,* (Washington D.C.: Municipal Reference Service Bureau of the Census, 1942).

- Parker-Hanson, E., *Transformation: The History of Modern Puerto Rico,* (New York: Simon and Schuster Publishers, 1955).

- Perusse, R.L., *The United States and Puerto Rico: Decolonisation Options and Prospects,* (Lanham/New York/London: University Press of America, Inc., 1987).

- Perusse, R.I., *The United States and Puerto Rico: The Struggle for Equality,* (Malabar: E.Krieger Publishing Company, 1990).

- Petrullo, V., *The Puerto Rican Paradox,* (Philadelphia/London: University of Pennsylvania Press, 1947).

- Reisman, W.M., *Puerto Rico and the International Process: New Roles in Association* (New York: West Publishing Company, 1973).

- Rivera Batiz, F.L., and Santiago, C., *Island of Paradox: Puerto Rico in the 1990s,* (New York: Russell Sage Foundation, 1996).

- Rodríguez, C.E., *Puerto Ricans Born in the U.S.A.,* (Boston/London/ Sydney/Wellington: Unwin Hyman, 1989).

- Rowe, L.S., *The United States and Puerto Rico,* (New York: Arno Press, 1975).

- Sánchez, V.E., *From Colonia to Community: The History of Puerto Ricans in New York City, 1917-1948,* (New York: International Publishers, 1980).

- Santuallano, L., *Mirada al Caribe: Fricción de Culturas en Puerto Rico* (Ciudad de Méjico: Editorial Jornadas, 1945).

- Sariola, S., *The Puerto Rican Dilemma,* (Port Whasington/London: National University Publications, 1979).

- Silén, J.A., *We, the Puerto Rican People: A Story of Oppression and Resistance,* (New York/London: Editorial Edil, Inc., 1971). Translated by Cedric Belfrage

- Smith, C.J., *Estructuras Políticas de Puerto Rico, 1940-1972* (San Juan de Puerto Rico: Editorial San Juan, 1973).

- Stead, W.H., *Fomento: The Economic Development of Puerto Rico* (Washington, D.C.: National Planning Association, 1958).

- Steiner, S., *The Islands: The Worlds of the Puerto Ricans,* (New York/London/San Francisco/Evanston: Harper and Row, 1974).

- Tata, R.J., *Structural Changes in Puerto Rico's Economy, 1947-1976,* (Athens: Ohio University Press, 1980).

- Trías Monge, J., *Puerto Rico: The Trials of the Oldest Colony in the World,* (New Haven: Yale University Press, 1997).

- Tugwell, R.G., *The Stricken Land: The Story of Puerto Rico,* (New York: Doubleday and Company, Inc., 1947).

- Wagenheim, K., *A Survey of Puerto Rican in the US Mainland in the 1970s,* (New York/ Washington/London: Praeger Publishers, 1975).

- _____, *Puerto Rico: A Profile,* (London: Pall Mall Press, 1970).

- _____, *Puerto Ricans in the United States,* (New York/London: Minority Rights Group, 1983).

- Weissfoff, RI, *Factories and Food Stamps: The Puerto Rico Model of Development,*(Baltimore/London: Hopkins University Press, 1985).

- Wells, H., *The Modernisation of Puerto Rico* (Cambridge: Harvard University Press, 1969).

- Williams, B., *Puerto Rico: Commonwealth, State or Nation?* (New York: Parent's Magazine Press, 1972)

- Zavala, I. and Rodriguez, R. (eds), *The Intellectual Roots of Independence,* (New York/ London: Monthly Review Press, 1980).

Articles

- Lizette Alvarez, "A Neighbourhood of Homesteaders: Hispanic Settlers Transform Harding Park in Bronx", *The New York Times*, December 31, 1996.

- Sam Roberts, "New York's Puerto Ricans Split in Economic Success", *The New York Times*, December 18, 1993.

Journals

- Henry Williams, "Puerto Rico: A New Constitution in America", *The Journal of Politics*, Vol. XV (October, 1953): 42.

Government Papers

- Comisión de Reorganización de la Rama Ejecutiva, *Estudio de las Operaciones y Situación Económica de las Corporaciones Públicas* (San Juan: Estado Libre Asociado de Puerto Rico, 1979).

- Department of the Treasury, *Puerto Rico: Report on Finances and Economy* (San Juan: Commonwealth of Puerto Rico, 1957).

- Governor Papers, *Report of the United States- Puerto Rico Commission on the Status of Puerto Rico* (Washington D.C.: U.S. Government Printing Office, 1966).

- Junta de Planificación de Puerto Rico, *Anuario Estadístico de Puerto Rico, 1970* (San Juan: Estado Libre Asociado de Puerto Rico, 1973).

- Junta de Planificación de Puerto Rico, *Anuario Estadístico de Puerto Rico, 1974* (San Juan: Estado Libre Asociado de Puerto Rico, 1976).

- Junta de Planificación de Puerto Rico, *Compedio de Estadísticas Sociales, 1988* (San Juan: Estado Libre Asociado de Puerto Rico, 1990).

- Junta de Planificación de Puerto Rico, *La Población Immigrante en Puerto Rico* (San Juan: Estado Libre Asociado de Puerto Rico, 1980).

- Junta de Planificación de Puerto Rico, *Serie Histórica del Empleo, Desempleo y Grupo Trabajador en Puerto Rico* (San Juan: Estado Libre Asociado de Puerto Rico, 1990).

- U.S. Government, *Text of the Constitution of the Commonwealth of Puerto Rico* (Washington D.C.: U.S. Government Printing Office, 1952).

Notes

[i] Reisman, M., *Puerto Rico and the International Process: New Roles in Association. A Report for the Conference on Puerto Rico and Foreign Policy Progress* (New York: West Publishing Company, 1975), 1.

[ii] There was 1 delegate for every 25 eligible voters. In order to be considered to vote, Puerto Ricans had to be male and 21 years of age or over.

[iii] Perusse, R.I., *The United States and Puerto Rico: The Struggle for Equality*, (Malabar: E. Krieger Publishing Company, 1990), 80.

[iv] Curet, E., *Puerto Rico: Development by Integration to the U.S.*, (Río Piedras: Editorial Cultural, 1986), 29.

[v] Wells, H., *The Modernisation of Puerto Rico*, (Cambridge: Harvard University Press, 1969), 87.

[vi] Wells, H., *The Modernisation of Puerto Rico*, (Cambridge: Harvard University Press, 1969), 89.

[vii] Perusse, R.L., *The United States and Puerto Rico: The Struggle for Equality*, (Malabar: E. Krieger Publishing company, 1990), 161.

[viii] Perusse, R.I., *The United States and Puerto Rico: The Struggle for Equality*, (Malabar: E. Krieger Publishing company, 1990), 17.

[ix] Williams, B., *Puerto Rico: Commonwealth, State or Nation?*,(New York: Parent's Magazine Press, 1972), 191.

[x] Williams, B., *Puerto Rico: Commonwealth, State or Nation?*,(New York: Parent's Magazine Press, 1972), 98.

[xi] López A., and Petras, J., *Puerto Rico and Puerto Ricans: Studies in History and society*, (New York/London/Sydney/Toronto: Schenkman Publishing Company, 1974), 217.

[xii] Williams, B., *Puerto Rico: Commonwealth, States or Nation?*, (New York: Parent's Magazine Press, 1972), 161.

[xiii] Petrullo, V., *The Puerto Rican Paradox*, (Philadelphia/London: University of Pennsylvania Press, 1947), 112.

[xiv] Chase, S., *"Operation Bootstrap" in Puerto Rico: Report of Progress*, (Washington, D.C.: the National Planning Association Business committee on National Policy, September 1951, Vol. 75), 15.

[xv] Curet, E., *Puerto Rico: Development by Integration to the U.S.*, (Río Piedras: Editorial Cultural, 1986), 31.

[xvi] Pagan, B., *Puerto Rico: The Next State*, (Washington, D.C.: Municipal Reference Service Bureau of the Census, 1942), 40.

[xvii] Curet, E., *El Desarrollo Económico de Puerto Rico,*, (San Juan: Management Aid Centre, Inc., 1976), 36.

[xviii] Stead, W.H., *Fomento: The Economic Development of Puerto Rico*, (Washington, D.C.: National Planning Association, 1958), 55.

[xix] Wagenheim, K., *Puerto Rico: A Profile*, (London: Pall Mall Press, 1970), 98.

[xx] Holbik, K.,and Swan, P.L., *Industralisation and Employment in Puerto Rico, 1950-1972*, (Austin: the University of texas, 1975), 15.

[xxi] Curet, E., *Puerto Rico: Development by Integration to the U.S.*, (Río Piedras: Editorial Cultural, 1986), 29.

[xxii] Wagenheim, K., *Puerto Rico: A Profile*, (London: Pall Mall Press, 1970), 112.

[xxiii] Holbik, K.,and Swan, P.L., *Industralisation and Employment in Puerto Rico, 1950-1972*, (Austin: the University of Texas, 1975), 18.

[xxiv] Reisman, W.M., *Puerto Rico and the International Process: New Roles in Association*, (New York: West Publishing Company, 1973), 30.

[xxv] Curet, E., *Puerto Rico: Development by Integration to the U.S.*, (Río Piedras: Editorial Cultural, 1986),26.

[xxvi] Holbik, K.,and Swan, P.L., *Industralisation and Employment in Puerto Rico, 1950-1972*, (Austin: the University of texas, 1975), 37.

[xxvii] Curet, E., *El Desarrollo Económico de Puerto Rico,*, (San Juan: Management Aid Centre, Inc., 1976), 318.

[xxviii] Sariola, S., *The Puerto Rican Dilemma*, (Port Washington/London: National University Publications, 1979), 133.

[xxix] Fitzpatrick, J.P., *Puerto Rican Americans: The Meaning of the Migration to the Mainland*, (New Jersey: J.P. Prentice-Hall Inc., 1987), 21.

[xxx] López A., and Petras, J., *Puerto Rico and Puerto Ricans: Studies in History and Society*, (New York/London/Sydney/Toronto: Schenkman Publishing Company, 1974), 157.

[xxxi] Rodríguez, C.E., *Puerto Ricans born in the U.S.A.*, (Boston/London/Sydney/Wellington: Unwin Hyman, 1989), 140.

[xxxii] Fitzpatrick, J.P., *Puerto Rican Americans: The Meaning of the Migration to the Mainland*, (New Jersey: J.P. Prentice-Hall Inc., 1987), 2.

[xxxiii] Fitzpatrick, J.P., *Puerto Rican Americans: The Meaning of the Migration to the Mainland*, (New Jersey: J.P. Prentice-Hall Inc., 1987), 92.

[xxxiv] Rodríguez, C.E., *Puerto Ricans born in the U.S.A.*, (Boston/London/Sydney/Wellington: Unwin Hyman, 1989): 116.

[xxxv] The Nationalist Party had a charismatic leader, Pedro Albizú Campos, who defended the idea that Puerto Rico had been illegally invaded as, at the time the Spanish-American peace treaty was signed, the Puerto Rican Chapter of Autonomy had entered into effect. Although under this Chapter, Puerto Rico could participate in international treaties that affected the island, Puerto Ricans were not invited to the peace table. During the 1930s, the Nationalists were responsible for numerous acts of terrorism and violence. The most significant of them was the killing of the American Chief of the Puerto Rican police, E. Francis Riggs, in 1936. Riggs' assassination resulted in Senator Millard Tyding, friend of Riggs, introducing to Congress the first of a series of pro-Puerto Rico independence bills, which became known as the Tyding Bills. The bill proposed a referendum on independence or statehood. In the case that the Puerto Ricans chose independence, a 4-year transition period would be implemented. It was the first time that independence was officially proposed by an American politician.

[xxxvi] In July 1946, the Puerto Rican Resident Commissioner in Washington, Jesus T. Piñero, was appointed by President Truman as the Puerto Rican Governor to the island.

xxxvii The English translation for Estado Libre Asociado is Free Associated State and not Commonwealth State as it was translated. This wrong translation of Puerto Rico's status would be the cause of numerous disputes between the United States' Congress and the Puerto Rican legislature.

xxxviii Morales Carrión, A., *Puerto Rico: A Political and Cultural History,* (New York: W.W. Norton and company, Inc., 1983), 278..

xxxix López A., and Petras, J., *Puerto Rico and Puerto Ricans: Studies in History and Society,* (New York/London/Sydney/Toronto: Schenkman Publishing Company, 1974), 156.

xl Morales Carrión, A., *Puerto Rico: A Political and Cultural History,* (New York: W.W. Norton and company, Inc., 1983), 306.

xli Perusse, R.I., *The United States and Puerto Rico: The Struggle for Equality,* (Malabar: E. Krieger Publishing company, 1990), 41.

xlii Ibid., 42.

xliii Perusse, R.I., *The United States and Puerto Rico: The Struggle for Equality,* (Malabar: E. Krieger Publishing company, 1990), 49.

xliv Perusse, R.I., *The United States and Puerto Rico: The Struggle for Equality,* (Malabar: E. Krieger Publishing company, 1990), 161.

xlv Reisman, W.M., *Puerto Rico and the International Process: New Roles in Association,* (New York: West Publishing Company, 1973), 12.

xlvi Falk, P.S., *The Political Status of Puerto Rico,* (Lexington/Toronto: Lexington Books, 1986), 19.

xlvii Fitzpatrick, J.P., *Puerto Rican Americans: The Meaning of the Migration to the Mainland,* (New Jersey: J.P. Prentice-Hall Inc., 1987), 35.

xlviii Rivera Batiz, F.L. and Santiago, C.E., *Island Paradox: Puerto Rico in the 1990s* (New York: Russell Sage Foundation, 1990), 3.

xlix Falk, P.S., *The Political Status of Puerto Rico,* (Lexington/Toronto: Lexington Books, 1986), 19.

l Ibid., 50.

[li] Petrullo, V., *The Puerto Rican Paradox*, (Philadelphia/London: University of Pennsylvania Press, 1947), 84.

[lii] Rivera Batiz, F.L. and Santiago, C.E., *Island Paradox: Puerto Rico in the 1990s* (New York: Russell Sage Foundation, 1990), 19.

[liii] Junta de Planificación de Puerto Rico, *Compedio de Estadísticas Sociales, 1988* (San Juan: Estado Libre Asociado de Puerto Rico, 1990), 20.

[liv] Junta de Planificación de Puerto Rico, *La Población Immigrante de Puerto Rico* (San Juan: Estado Libre Asociado de Puerto Rico, 1980), 12.

[lv] Curet, E., *Puerto Rico: Development by Integration to the U.S.*, (Río Piedras: Editorial Cultural, 1986), 72.

[lvi] Curet, E., *Puerto Rico: Development by Integration to the U.S.*, (Río Piedras: Editorial Cultural, 1986), 47.